The Way
of the
Cross

Juliette Levivier

Illustrations by Anne Gravier

MAGNIFICAT · Ignatius

Table
of Contents

Holy Week

Jesus went to Jerusalem to celebrate the Passover as he did every year. This year though, when he entered the city with his disciples, a large crowd came out to meet him shouting, "Hosanna! Blessed is he who comes in the name of the Lord!"

IT IS PALM SUNDAY.

A few days later, while he was sharing his last meal with his disciples, Jesus took the bread and said to them, "Take this, all of you, and eat of it, for this is my Body, which will *be* given up for you."

Then he took the cup and said to them, "Take this, all of you, and drink from it, for this is the chalice of my Blood, which will *be* poured out for you and for many for the forgiveness of sins."

IT IS HOLY THURSDAY.

A little later, during the night, Jesus was arrested while he was praying in the Garden of Gethsemane. He was brought before the court and condemned to death.

Then he was whipped and insulted. They mocked him, putting a crown made of thorns on his head and dressing him in a King's cloak.

Then he was led to a hill, not far from the city, to be crucified.

At three o'clock in the afternoon, Jesus died on the cross.

After his death, his friends placed his body in a tomb.

IT IS GOOD FRIDAY.

Jesus was dead.

Jesus, who had brought the love and peace of God his Father to all, who had never committed any sins, had been put to death as a criminal.

All those who loved him and who believed in him were very sad. They felt abandoned and lost.

IT IS HOLY SATURDAY.

Very early the next morning, some women, and then some disciples, went to the tomb. It was empty.

Jesus was not there anymore. He had risen from the dead!

Love has overcome violence and death.

IT IS EASTER MORNING!

Where the Way of the Cross Comes from

It was in Jerusalem that Jesus suffered his passion and died on the cross, giving his life for us to save us from sin.

It was there too, three days later, that he rose from death.

For centuries, Christians have gone on pilgrimage to Jerusalem to pray at the places where Jesus suffered, died and rose from the dead, following the same way Jesus walked as he carried his cross.

Christians who could not make the journey to Jerusalem made places in or near their churches where they too could follow the Way of the Cross.

That is the reason there is a Way of the Cross in every Catholic church.

Churches, monasteries and retreat centers sometimes have an outdoor Way of the Cross.

Our Faith
in the Resurrection

The Way of the Cross has fourteen stages called stations. Each one is represented by a picture or a statue or a simple wooden cross.

Some of the stations are episodes spoken of in the Gospels; others are not, but they come from a very old tradition.

The Way of the Cross ends with Jesus being laid in the tomb.

It would be very sad to stop there, because it's our faith in the Resurrection that accompanies us throughout the Way of the Cross.

That's why there is an optional fifteenth station for Easter morning.

Jesus Invites You to Follow Him

When you follow Jesus on the Way of the Cross, you can begin to see how incredible his love is for you.

By your prayer, you join in Jesus' suffering and in the suffering of all.

By your prayer, you thank Jesus. He endured everything for you and for each one of us.

When you pray the Way of the Cross, Jesus invites you to change your heart to love as he does.

For You!

You probably have noticed the Stations of the Cross in your parish church.

They are there for you!

Many Catholics pray the stations on Fridays, especially the Fridays of Lent.

On Good Friday there are often special services for praying the Way of the Cross. Some of these are held outdoors with crowds of people.

How to Pray
the Way of the Cross

Using the following pages as a guide, you can pray the Way of the Cross at church or at home.

1) Stand, sit or kneel.

2) Read the title of the station and say:

"We adore you, O Christ, and we praise you because by your holy Cross, you have redeemed the world."

3) Read the short passage from the Bible.

4) Read the lines that follow and study the picture. Try to imagine the scene. Look at Jesus. Look at the other people who are with him. What prayer comes into your heart?

5) Say the prayer under the picture.

Jesus Is Condemned to Death

*Having scourged Jesus,
Pilate delivered him to be crucified.*

Mark 15:15

How beautiful is Jesus' gentleness in the face of those who want to kill him.

How patient he is. How serene.

He answers calmly, but who believes he is the Son of God?

The religious leaders and the crowd demand his death. Pilate, the Roman governor, gives them what they want.

When I am judged unfairly,
and have no one to defend me,
help me, Jesus, to bear this patiently.
Teach me not to condemn others
but to forgive the way you do.

2nd

STATION

Jesus Carries His Cross

He went out, bearing his own cross.

John 19:17

How heavy Jesus' cross is! It wounds his shoulders already injured by the blows.

But Jesus carries it himself. He doesn't run away from suffering. He agrees to carry the weight of our sins along with his cross. He agrees to carry the weight of our sufferings along with his cross.

He agrees to carry the weight of our salvation along with his cross. That's how much he loves us.

O Jesus, you help me carry the weight
of the great and small sufferings of my life.
I pray to you, Lord,
for all those who are struggling
under the weight of difficulties,
injustice and all sorts of suffering.

Jesus Falls for the First Time

Come to me all who labor and are
heavy laden, and I will give you rest.

Matthew 11:28

Jesus is exhausted and the cross is so heavy, he falls beneath its weight. Humbly he stands up again and continues on his way.

It is our lies, our pride and our wickedness that make us fall.

Jesus lifts us up again. He takes our cross as well as his own. He strengthens us.

We are nothing without him.

O Jesus, give me your strength
   when I am discouraged and
   when everything is difficult.
   Help me to stand up again
and not stay crushed by my sadness.

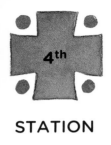

Jesus Meets His Mother, Mary

Simeon blessed them and said to Mary his mother, " . . . and a sword will pierce through your own soul also."

Luke 2:34-35

Mary is at the side of the road. She gives Jesus courage, and she accompanies him right to the end.

Their eyes meet, full of love for each other.

Just by being there, she helps him with the strength of her love.

Poor Mary—her heart is pierced with sorrow, but she is still full of hope because she knows Jesus is the Son of God.

Lord Jesus, I pray to you for all the children
of the world who are suffering in their bodies
or in their hearts and who don't have a mother
near them to comfort them.
May the Virgin Mary, your mother,
give them her tenderness.

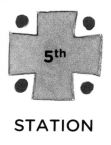

Simon of Cyrene Helps Jesus to Carry His Cross

They seized one Simon of Cyrene,
who was coming in from the country,
and laid on him the cross, to carry it behind Jesus.

Luke 23:26

Simon doesn't have a choice. He is pulled out of the crowd to help Jesus. But he has a good heart and he is touched by Jesus' suffering.

He helps Jesus as much by his compassion as by the strength of his arms.

Like Simon, we can help others to carry their burdens. We can soothe their hurts and comfort them when they are sad.

Lord Jesus,
do you need me to carry your cross?
Make me aware of people who need my help.
When I help them,
I am helping you.

6th STATION

Veronica Wipes the Face of Jesus

As one from whom men hide their faces
he was despised, and we esteemed him not.

Isaiah 53:3

Poor Jesus—he is battered, bruised and bleeding. His face is marked by pain and sorrow. Many turn away from him.

Here is lovely Veronica, full of goodness.

Jesus pauses, and she gently wipes his face.

In thanks for her kindness, Jesus leaves her with a gift: the image of his holy face on her cloth.

Jesus, I pray for the sick,
the old, the lonely and all those
who are abandoned in their suffering.
Help me to be like Veronica,
to reach out in whatever ways I can.

Jesus Falls
for the Second Time

He was oppressed, and he was afflicted . . .
like a lamb that is lead to the slaughter . . .
he opened not his mouth.

Isaiah 53:7

Jesus falls down exhausted.

The crowd murmurs. The soldiers are impatient.

Slowly, silently he gets up again and continues walking.

Our weaknesses and our bad habits often make us fall. It's Jesus' strength that lifts us up again.

Even if I make good resolutions,
I find it hard to keep them!
O Jesus, teach me not to become discouraged
and, when I fall, to accept it humbly.
Give me your patience
and your strength.

Jesus Meets the Women of Jerusalem

Jesus turning to them said, "Daughters of Jerusalem, do not weep for me, but weep for yourselves and for your children."

Luke 23:28

Along the road some women are crying and lamenting. When they see Jesus pass, exhausted, in front of them, they are filled with pity.

Jesus, forgetting his own suffering, breaks his silence to tell them to look at their sorrows, to open their hearts and to change their lives.

He invites us too to convert our hearts, our thoughts, our words and our actions.

You know, Lord, how much easier it is for me
to see the faults of others than to see my own!
Teach me to recognize my sins
and to follow the way of forgiveness.
Help me to come out of my selfishness
and to open my heart.

9th

STATION

Jesus Falls for the Third Time

Truly, truly, I say to you, unless a grain
of wheat falls into the earth and dies,
it remains alone; but if it dies,
it bears much fruit.

John 12:24

Three times Jesus falls under the weight of his cross. Three times he stands up again.

His strength fails him, but not his will. What a lesson in courage he teaches us!

Out of love for us, he goes to the end of the journey.

He does for us what we cannot do for ourselves.

In spite of all the times I fall, Lord,
I know you always love me.
Thank you, Jesus, for lifting me up again
and giving me the joy of your forgiveness
through the sacrament of Reconciliation.

10th

STATION

Jesus Is Stripped of His Clothes

They took his garments and made four parts,
one for each soldier.

John 19:23

All the people are shouting and jostling him. They mock him with their looks and insult him with their words. Their hearts are closed.

Jesus is stripped naked and humiliated. He does not complain. He does not defend himself.

In spite of their offenses and insults, he continues to love them. His dignity shines through.

Lord, you made us
in your image and likeness.
So many people suffer insults,
ridicule and outrage.
Jesus, you recognize their dignity
because you love them.
Teach me to look at the poor with love.

Jesus Is Nailed to the Cross

*When Jesus saw his mother, and the disciple
whom he loved standing near,
he said to his mother,
"Woman, behold, your son!"
Then he said to the disciple,
"Behold, your mother!"*

John 19:26-27

See, Mary is still there near Jesus. She does not abandon him.

See, Jesus' feet are pierced through. Will you give him yours to spread the good news of God's love?

See, his hands are destroyed. Will you give him yours to serve your brothers?

See, Jesus' arms are open. Will you let his arms close around you?

Yes, Lord Jesus:
I will take Mary as my own mother.
With her, I will stand at the foot of the cross.
With her, I will pray that your love
will reach all men.

Jesus Dies on the Cross

When they came to the place
which is called the Skull,
there they crucified him . . . Jesus said,
"Father, forgive them; for they know not
what they are doing."

Luke 23:33-34

Jesus is dying. In spite of his suffering, Jesus speaks to his Father.

Listen to his prayer. He is calling on God's mercy because he has already forgiven those who are killing him.

He replies to their brutality with gentleness.

He replies to their hatred with love.

Listen to Jesus' cry at the moment of his death. It is a cry of suffering, but it is also a cry of love.

Lord Jesus,
at the hour of your death
your arms are wide open to welcome us
and to offer us your forgiveness.
Teach me, Jesus, to forgive others
as you forgive me.

Jesus Is Taken Down from the Cross

When it was evening, there came a rich man of Arimathea, named Joseph, who also was a disciple of Jesus. He went to Pilate and asked for the body of Jesus. Then Pilate ordered it to be given to him.

Matthew 27:57-58

Jesus is dead.

Mary is still there with John and some others.

There is Joseph of Arimathea, a friend of Jesus. His heart aches, and he is full of respect. He takes Jesus down from the cross and places him in Mary's arms. She holds him for the last time.

Mary prays as her son has taught her.

She cries, she prays, she loves us.

Mary, when you receive Jesus' body,
your pain is boundless,
but he gives you his peace.
Jesus, when I pray your peace dwells in me.
I want to live in that peace.

Jesus Is Laid in the Tomb

Joseph took the body,
and wrapped it in a clean linen shroud,
and laid it in his own new tomb . . .
and he rolled a great stone
to the door of the tomb,
and departed.

Matthew 27:59-60

Suddenly, there is only silence and emptiness.

Jesus is no longer seen, no longer heard. No one can touch him or speak to him.

The disciples of Jesus are full of grief. They feel lost and afraid. Not knowing what else to do, they wait and they pray.

Sometimes, Jesus, I am lonely.
Sometimes I feel sad or afraid.
In the silence of my heart,
help me to wait for you
and to listen for your voice.

Jesus Rises from the Dead

The angel said to the women,
"Do not be afraid; for I know
that you seek Jesus who was crucified.
He is not here; for he has risen, as he said."

Matthew 28:5-6

It is a beautiful Sunday morning when women return to the tomb on that first Easter.

It is springtime, when nature is reborn. The sun is shining, flowers are blooming, and birds are singing.

The women are amazed to find the tomb empty. An angel tells them that Jesus is alive, and full of joy they run quickly to tell the apostles.

O Jesus, make me a witness to your love.
May the glory of your Resurrection
light up my heart
and shine through my eyes,
breaking through
in all I say and do!

Cover illustration by Anne Gravier

Original French edition:
Le chemin de Croix

Printed by Pollina on December 4, 2012
Job Number MGN 12017
Printed in France, in compliance with the Consumer Protection Safety Act of 2008.